Lazily, Crazily, Just a Bit Nasally

More about Adverbs

To Brendan
—B.P.C.

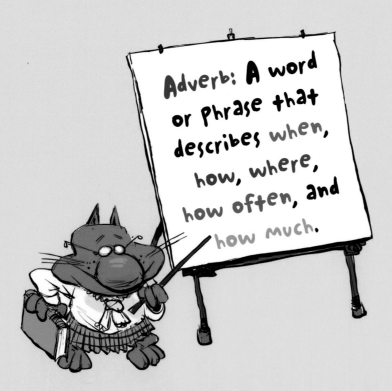

Adverb: A word or phrase that describes when, how, where, how often, and how much.

The adverbs in this book are color coded. The colors of the words on this page match the colors of the adverbs in the text. You'll see that all pink adverbs tell you when, all green adverbs tell you how often, and so on. Watch out for adverbs that tell you how. Some are light blue and others are dark blue.

Lazily, Crazily, Just a Bit Nasally

More about Adverbs

by Brian P. Cleary

illustrations by Brian Gable

M MILLBROOK PRESS / MINNEAPOLIS

Adverbs sometimes tell us where,

like these are here and those are there.

4

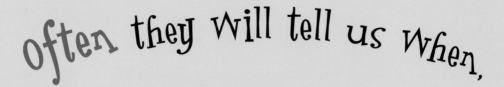

often they will tell us when,

like this is now and
that was then.

Adverbs sometimes tell us how,

like, "carefully remove this cow."

They let us know how often too,

as in the phrase, "I seldom chew."

At times they modify the verb,

as in, "He slowly paints the curb."

Cheerily, she rose from bed.

Eerily, he stared ahead.

Lazily sleeping,
nasally weeping,
a dude eating food
while he's rudely beep-beeping.

Crazily, Curtis repainted the Chang bridge.

THE CHANG RIVER BRIDGE

Adverbs add all kinds of life to our language!

They help give
adjectives a boost,

as in, "This price is
quite reduced!"

SALE
$10.00
1¢

Very pretty,

wryly funny,

dismally dark,

and blindingly sunny.

Sometimes "how much" is the question they answer,

as in, "she's a totally terrible dancer."

Partially stubborn,

barely polite,

hardly been fed on
this awfully cold night.

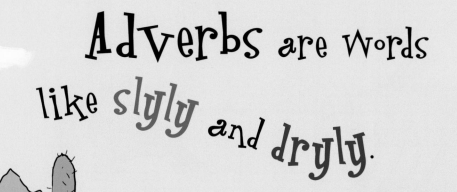

Adverbs are words like slyly and dryly.

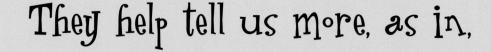

They help tell us more, as in,

"He answered shyly."

Daringly,

dashingly,

darkly,

directly—

you guessed these were **adverbs?**

Then you guessed correctly!

So are bleakly,

blandly,

weakly,

coolly, newly, somewhat chicly.

18

Terribly, tauntingly,
hauntingly spoken,

frantically,

forcibly,

physically broken.

Sometimes adverbs come in phrases,

like, for a while, she built these mazes.

20

In the meantime,
he got
lost.

Here and
there,

you'll find
some frost.

If you said these terms
are all **adverbs** of time,

I'll tell you right now that you're right!

If we had no **adverbs,**
then we couldn't say
that this was done neatly

or sweetly.

We couldn't say loosely
or rather obtusely.

We'd describe things
a bit less completely.

We couldn't say Natalie,
acting quite brattily,

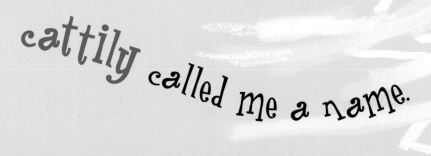

cattily called me a name.

We couldn't say, chattily, nastily,
Natalie rottenly ruined our game.

So write all the **adverbs** you know on a page.

Write sloppily,

HuGeLY,

or tinily.

Boastfully, blissfully, make out a list for me. You've learned What an **adverb** is—finally!

So, what is an adverb?

Do you know?

Find activities, games, and more at
www.brianpcleary.com

ABOUT THE AUTHOR & ILLUSTRATOR

BRIAN P. CLEARY is the author of the best-selling Words Are CATegorical® series, as well as the Math Is CATegorical®, Sounds Like Reading™ and Adventures in Memory™ series, The Laugh Stand: Adventures in Humor, Peanut Butter and Jellyfishes: A Very Silly Alphabet Book, Rainbow Soup: Adventures in Poetry, and Rhyme & PUNishment: Adventures in Wordplay. Mr. Cleary lives in Cleveland, Ohio.

BRIAN GABLE is the illustrator of several Words Are CATegorical® books, as well as the Math Is CATegorical® series. Mr. Gable also works as a political cartoonist for the Globe and Mail newspaper in Toronto, Canada.

Text copyright © 2008 by Brian P. Cleary
Illustrations copyright © 2008 by Lerner Publishing Group, Inc.

Millbrook Press
A division of Lerner Publishing Group, Inc.
241 First Avenue North
Minneapolis, MN 55401 U.S.A.

Website address: www.lernerbooks.com

Library of Congress Cataloging-in-Publication Data

Cleary, Brian P., 1959–
    Lazily, crazily, just a bit nasally: more about adverbs / by Brian P. Cleary ; illustrations by Brian Gable.
        p.   cm. — (Words are categorical)
    ISBN-13: 978–0–8225–7848–2 (lib. bdg. : alk. paper)
    1. English language—Adverb—Juvenile literature. I. Gable, Brian, 1949– ill. II. Title.
PE1325.C58 2008
428.2—dc22
                                                                    2006033800

Manufactured in the United States of America
3 — JR — 12/31/09